TAKE THE LEAD

PIANO

Grease

In the book	Page no.	On the CD	
		Demonstration	Backing
Greased Lightnin'	**10**	Track ⑤	Track ⑥
Beauty School Dropout	**2**	Track ①	Track ②
Look At Me, I'm Sandra Dee	**22**	Track ⑪	Track ⑫
Summer Nights	**15**	Track ⑦	Track ⑧
It's Raining On Prom Night	**7**	Track ③	Track ④
We Go Together	**25**	Track ⑬	Track ⑭
There Are Worse Things I Could Do	**19**	Track ⑨	Track ⑩
You're The One That I Want	**32**	Track ⑮	Track ⑯

Series Editor: Anna Joyce

Editorial, production and recording: Artemis Music Limited • Design and production: Space DPS Limited • Published 2002

IMP

International
MUSIC
Publications

Beauty School Dropout

Demonstration

Backing

Words and Music by
Jim Jacobs and Warren Casey

Slowly

Moderately (in 2)

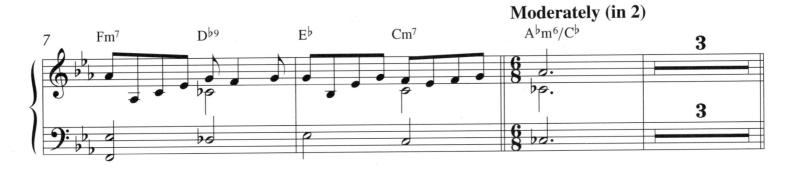

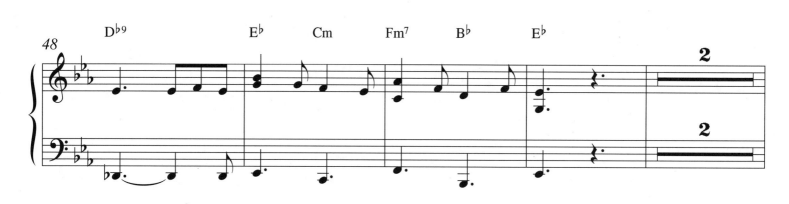

93
B♭
C
F
F(♯5)
97
B♭
E♭9
F
Dm
Gm7
C
102
F
2
Dm
mp
F
Dm
108
F
Dm
F
Dm
F
113
Dm
F
Dm
F

It's Raining On Prom Night

Demonstration

Backing

Words and Music by
Jim Jacobs and Warren Casey

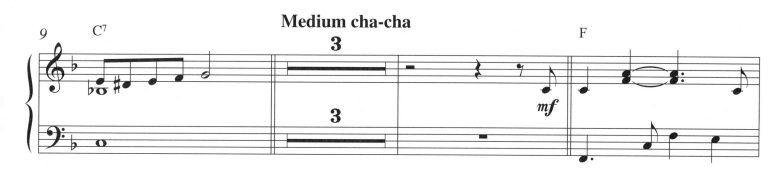

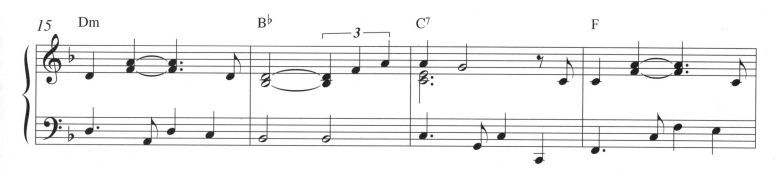

Greased Lightnin'

Words and Music by
Jim Jacobs and Warren Casey

Fast rock 'n' roll beat

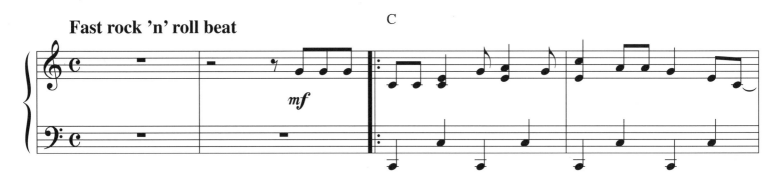

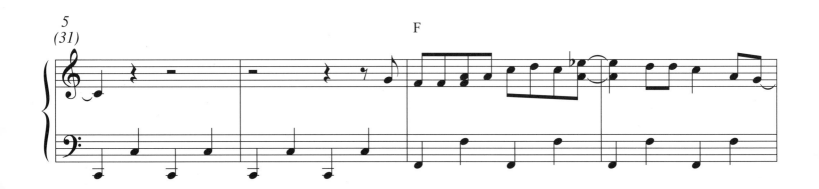

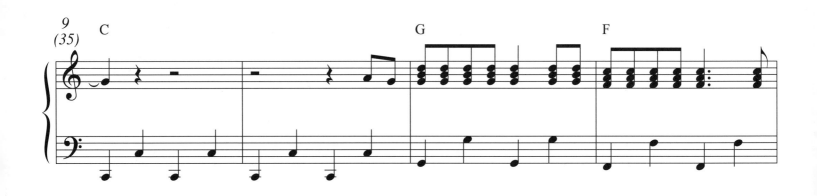

Summer Nights

Demonstration Backing

Words and Music by
Jim Jacobs and Warren Casey

Moderately

There Are Worse Things I Could Do

Demonstration   Backing

Words and Music by
Jim Jacobs and Warren Casey

Look At Me, I'm Sandra Dee

Demonstration

Backing

Words and Music by
Jim Jacobs and Warren Casey

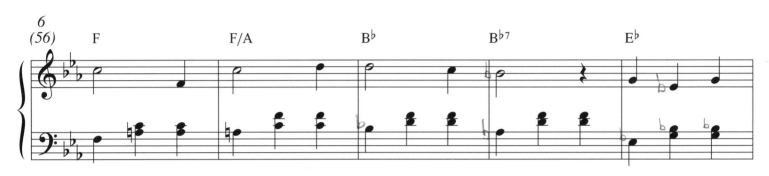

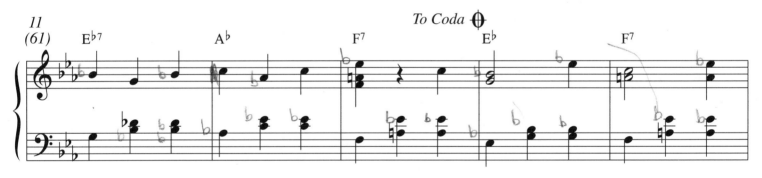

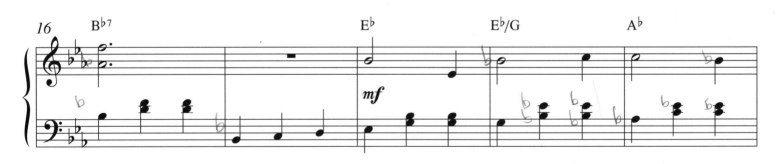

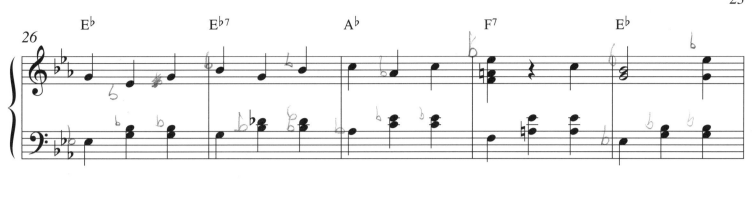

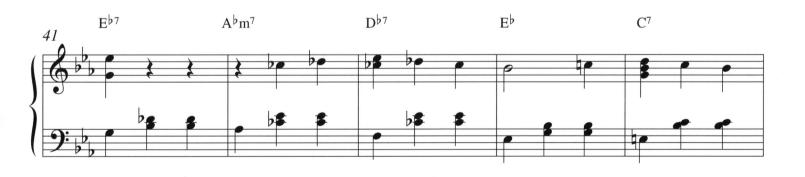

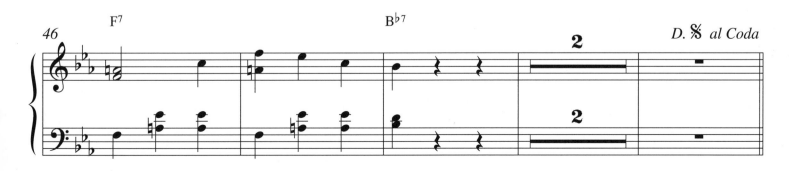

⊕ CODA

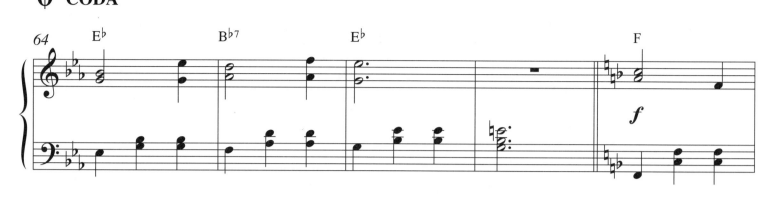

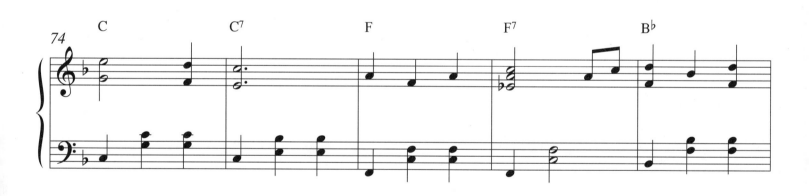

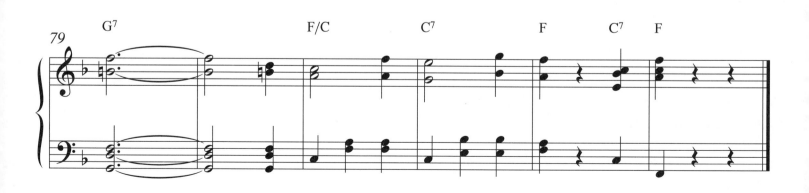

We Go Together

Words and Music by
Jim Jacobs and Warren Casey

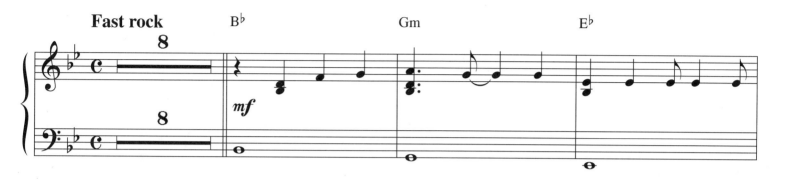

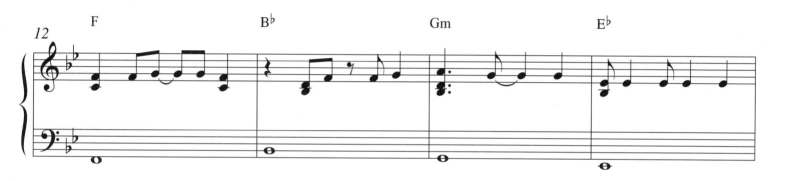

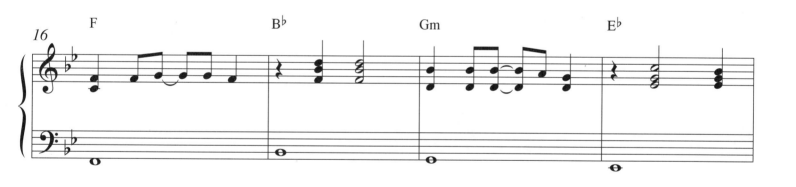

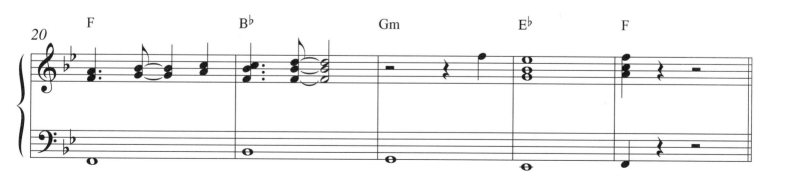

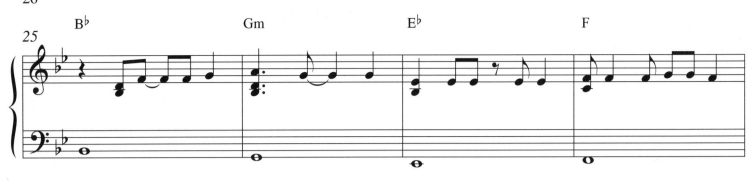

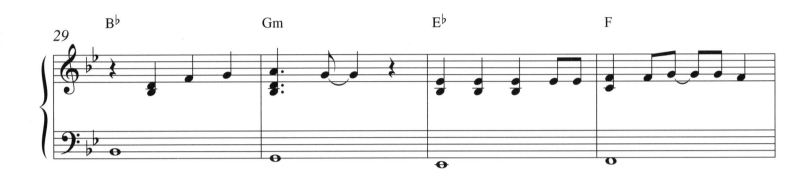

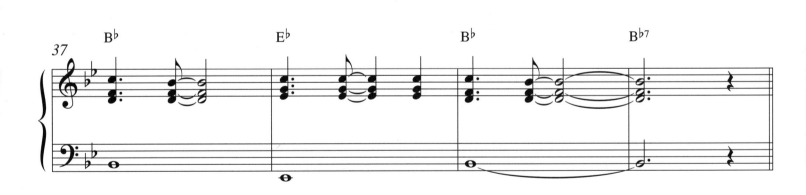

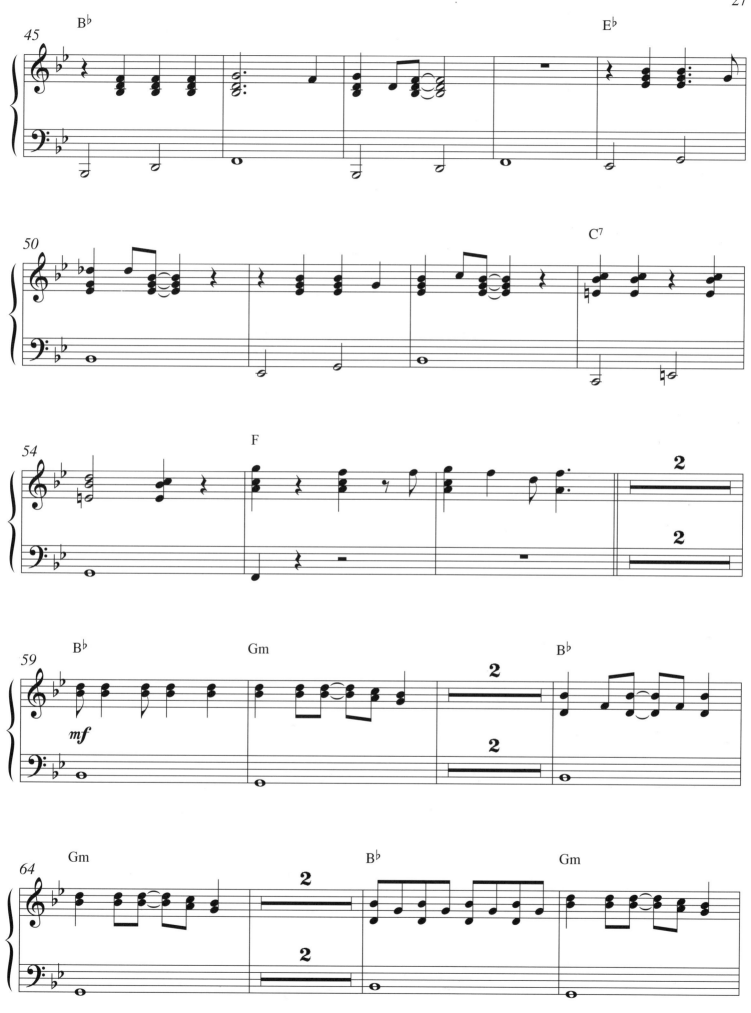

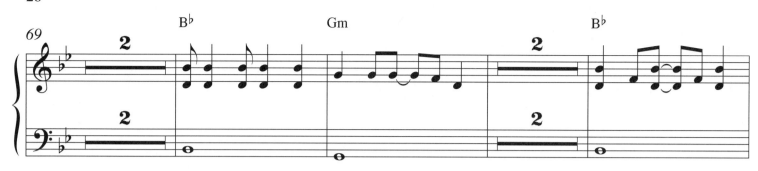

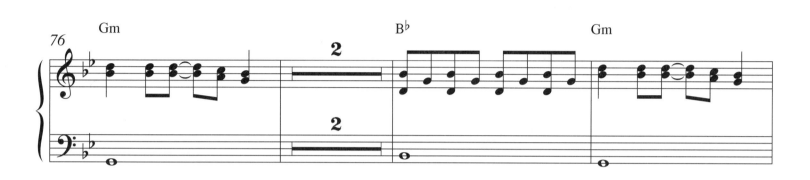

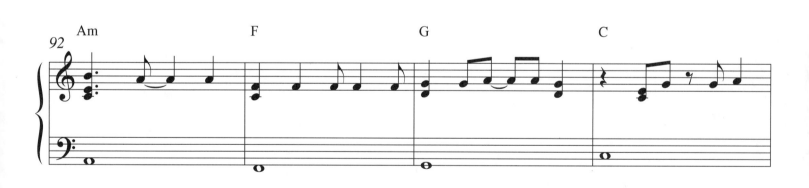

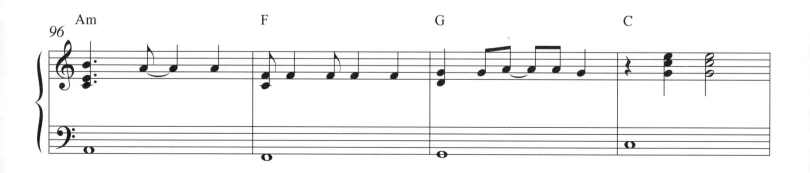

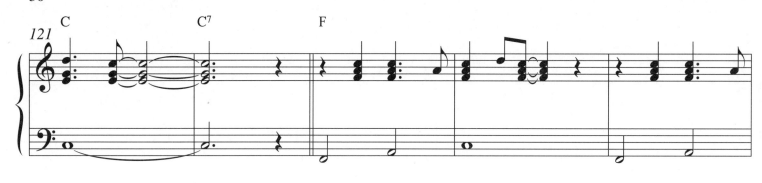

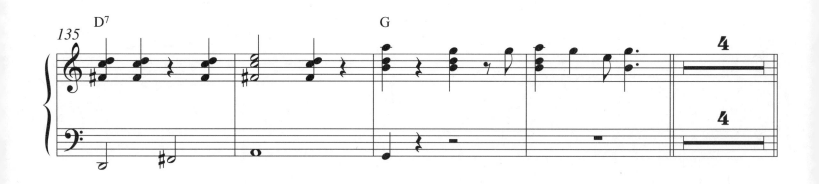

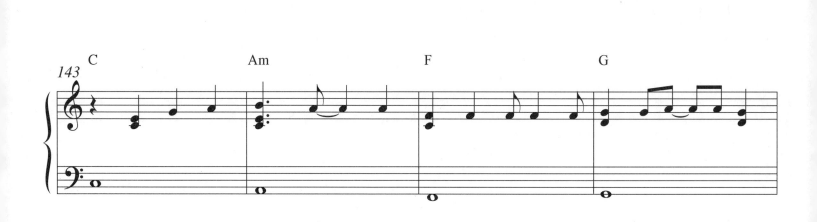

You're The One That I Want

Demonstration

Backing

Words and Music by John Farrar

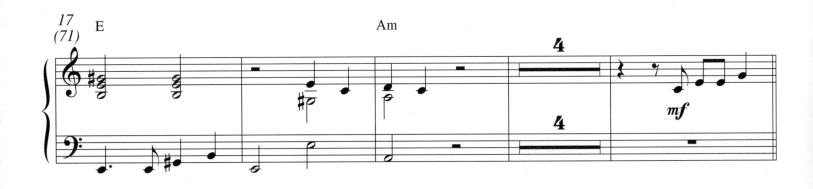

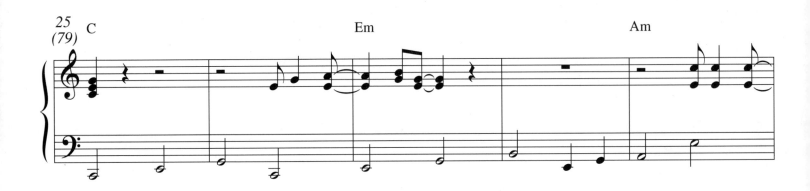

An expansive series of over 50 titles!

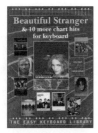

Beautiful Stranger
& 10 More Chart Hits
Ref: 7016A
ISBN: 1-85909-763-4

Big Band Hits
Ref: 19098
ISBN: 1-85909-142-3

Big Collection One
Ref: 5773A
ISBN: 1-85909-642-5

Big Collection Two
Ref: 5774A
ISBN: 1-85909-643-3

Big Collection Three
Ref: 5775A
ISBN: 1-85909-644-1

Blues
Ref: 3477A
ISBN: 1-85909-315-9

Celebration Songs
Ref: 3478A
ISBN: 1-85909-316-7

Christmas Carols
Ref: 4616A
ISBN: 1-85909-420-1

Christmas Songs
Ref: 19198
ISBN: 1-85909-173-3

Classic Hits One
Ref: 19099
ISBN: 1-85909-143-1

Classic Hits Two
Ref: 19100
ISBN: 1-85909-144-X

Country Songs
Ref: 19101
ISBN: 1-85909-145-8

Essential Chord Dictionary
Ref: 5776A
ISBN: 1-85909-683-2

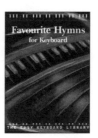

Favourite Hymns
Ref: 4179A
ISBN: 1-85909-380-9

Film Classics
Ref: 19197
ISBN: 1-85909-172-5

Glenn Miller
Ref: 5772A
ISBN: 1-85909-552-6

Great Songwriters
Ref: 2225A
ISBN: 1-85909-199-7

Whitney Houston
Ref: 7647A
ISBN: 1-85909-961-0

Instrumental Classics
Ref: 2338A
ISBN: 1-85909-219-5

I Try
& 10 More Chart Hits
Ref: 5778A
ISBN: 1-85909-877-0

Jazz Classics
Ref: 5770A
ISBN: 1-85909-529-1

Elton John
Ref: 5779A
ISBN: 1-85909-936-X

Latin Collection
Ref: 5777A
ISBN: 1-85909-842-8

Love Songs One
Ref: 19102
ISBN: 1-85909-146-6

Love Songs Two
Ref: 19199
ISBN: 1-85909-174-1

George Michael
Ref: 7646A
ISBN: 1-85909-960-2

Each song features melody line, vocals, chord displays, suggested registrations and rhythm settings.

"For each title ALL the chords (both 3 finger and 4 finger) used are shown in the correct position - which makes a change!" **Organ & Keyboard Cavalcade, May 2001**

Each song appears on two facing pages eliminating the need to turn the page during performance. We have just introduced a new cover look to the series and will repackage the backlist in the same way.

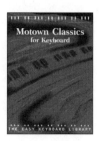

Motown Classics
Ref: 2337A
ISBN: 1-85909-218-7

Music Hall
Ref: 3329A
ISBN: 1-85909-309-4

Number One Hits
Ref: 19200
ISBN: 1-85909-175-X

Popular Classics
Ref: 4180A
ISBN: 1-85909-381-7

Pub Singalong Collection
Ref: 3954A
ISBN: 1-85909-370-1

Cliff Richard
Ref: 9030A
ISBN: 1-84328-032-9

Rock n Roll Classics
Ref: 2224A
ISBN: 1-85909-198-9

Showtunes One
Ref: 19103
ISBN: 1-85909-147-4

Showtunes Two
Ref: 3328A
ISBN: 1-85909-308-6

Frank Sinatra
Ref: 9025A
ISBN: 1-903692-15-6

Soft Rock Collection
Ref: 4617A
ISBN: 1-85909-421-X

Soul Classics
Ref: 19201
ISBN: 1-85909-176-8

The Twenties
Ref: 2969A
ISBN: 1-85909-268-3

The Thirties
Ref: 2970A
ISBN: 1-85909-269-1

The Forties
Ref: 2971A
ISBN: 1-85909-270-5

The Fifties
Ref: 2972A
ISBN: 1-85909-271-3

The Sixties
Ref: 2973A
ISBN: 1-85909-272-1

The Seventies
Ref: 2974A
ISBN: 1-85909-273-X

The Eighties
Ref: 2975A
ISBN: 1-85909-274-8

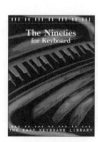

The Nineties
Ref: 2976A
ISBN: 1-85909-275-6

Traditional English
Favourites
Ref: 4229A
ISBN: 1-85909-398-1

Traditional Irish
Favourites
Ref: 4230A
ISBN: 1-85909-399-X

Traditional Scottish
Favourites
Ref: 4231A
ISBN: 1-85909-400-7

TV Themes
Ref: 19196
ISBN: 1-85909-171-7

Wartime Collection
Ref: 3955A
ISBN: 1-85909-371-X

Wedding Collection
Ref: 3688A
ISBN: 1-85909-334-5

14. Young at Heart

2. Becalmed

backing - track 2
performance - track 12

Christopher Norton